THE SPOKEN TRUTH

LIFE WRITTEN IN POETRY

Marcus L. Harvey

The Spoken Truth
Life Written in Poetry
Marcus L. Harvey, MBA

Copyright © 2022 by Marcus Harvey.

All rights reserved. Printed in the United States of America. No part of this book may be used or reproduced in any manner whatsoever without written permission, except in the case of brief quotations embodied in critical articles or reviews. Library of Congress cataloging-in-publication data has been applied for.
ISBN: 979-8-218-10224-1

1-11867281591

Dedication

This book is dedicated to the memory of my big brother Antonio Miguel Harvey. My big brother has always been my inspiration. As you look down upon me Big Bro, I will continue to make you proud. Love you and miss you tremendously.

Dear Reader

Thank you for coming on this journey with me. This book is a collection of poems I have written over several years, throughout various times in my life. I bare my soul through this artwork in the representation of spirituality, cultural perspective, and plain old life experience. I pray you find something between these pages that connects our human experiences. I deeply appreciate you for the moments in time you have taken to digest every thought, emotion, and experience I so happily and willfully share with you. May blessings be upon you for an eternity!

CONTENTS

CHAPTER 1 — 1

I Need My Truth	2
Living to Be A Better Me	6
Not Everything is for You	7
Cry Baby Blues	8
The Stand Against Us	9
Thinking Human, Humans Thinking	10
Power In Me	11

CHAPTER 2 — 12

His Story, Our Pain	13
We Conquered Happiness	16
Let's Connect	17
Love Yourself To Life	18
We Spirits of the Galaxies	19
Rise Up Human	21
Rebels or Revolutionaries	22
Love is Serious	24
First Glance	25
Love Me or Miss Me	26
Nature's Song And Dance	27

CHAPTER 3 — 28

Thank You Letter — 29
Open Arms — 31
Standing in the Rain — 32
Momma Ain't Playing — 33
Straight Talk Please — 35
You Dirty Cheater — 37
Be Yourself — 38
Directions Please — 40
I'm Not Perfect; I'm Strong — 41
Too Much Noise — 42

CHAPTER 4 — 43

Victims Don't Die, We Survive To Fight — 44
Confessions of A Human — 45
Gaslighting My Love — 46
My Dedication — 47
Don't Forget Me — 48
Where I'm From. — 49
Objects of Desire — 51
I Can See That — 53
I Will Argue With Me Until I'm Better — 54
The Power In Me — 56

CHAPTER 5 — 57

I Can't Hate You — 58
Nobody Is Perfect — 59

Message to My People	60
Taking Responsibility	62
Looking For Love & Finding Love Addiction	64
Message to You Reading This.	65
We Sure Love Our Jobs Don't We?	66
Message to the Oppressed	67
We Are Scared of the Law	69

CHAPTER 6 — 72

I Wrote You A Letter	73
I Saw The Truth	74
A Bit Too Heavy	75
Smile, Please	76
Sun Rise	77
Thank You Prayer	79
Something About Time	80
Them Good Ol' Church Days.	82
Message From My Ancestors Through Me to You.	84

CHAPTER 7 — 86

Days of Our Lives	87
That Old Piano Playing Life's Tunes	89
Love At First Sight	91
Surviving The Breakup	93
Humans United Defying and Ignoring Differences	95
Voices of Generations	98
You Can't Hide Pain, So Ask for Help	100
Message to Ourselves	101

CHAPTER 8   **102**

Soundtrack for Movement	103
Building Self Esteem	105
I Remember Words of The Ancestors	107
I'm Only Human	108
COVID Had Me Tripping	109
Peace Upon the Earth Children	111
The Flight	113
Finding Another Truth	115

Chapter 1

I Need My Truth

Dear Truth,
Greetings and salutations,
I've been waiting
To hear from you.
Every time I try to connect,
I don't get through.
I've been feeling concerned;
Plus, I really miss you,
Especially with
All we been through.
I reached out a few times
When everyone ignored you;
I got no answer.
I don't know what to do:
How can I live without you?
I can't live without my truth.
The best of me,
It is based on you.
The few times we spoke
Over the last few weeks
Felt so insincere.
It was way too brief.
I said my piece

And got no response.
I know you say it's
Not my fault.
If I'm being honest,
I feel like my
Integrity has been bought.
I caught them
Ignoring you,
And I said nothing.
I'll be honest.
This is hard to stomach.
They should show respect
When they see you coming.
Instead, they just
Turn their heads
And watch you plummet.
There is no excuse,
No time to be humble
I've got to take this stand.
This separation between
You and I,
I will no longer stand.
I need you, Truth.
You're my everything.
You are in everything I do;
You're the reason I breathe.
I'm so in love with you.
What should I do to
Prove this very fact?

The Spoken Truth

What I said the last time
We spoke,
I'll take it back.
No more innuendos.
From now on,
It's only facts.
Everything I ever spoke
Against you,
I take it all back.
I just want us to be us again.
Nothing in between us.
No more spins.
No more conversations
That led to dead ends.
If I say it again,
Then I mean it.
So, give me another chance.
Believe it when I say
I do.
Meaning I stand for you,
The whole truth
And nothing but the truth.
Simply because I love you.
If I may start with the past,
I promise you a present.
If the problem is now,
Let's get ahead of it
So now you see
The past is relevant.

Don't judge the new me:
The old me was reckless.
The old me connected
With the most benevolent.
Now, each thought pattern
Becomes more relevant.
I become we;
Self becomes selfless.
You still don't get it.
Beyond your filthy rhetoric
Lies the truth.
Lies told to you
Was given to me too.
Married to the pain?
Yes, I do.
The pain lives on
Because I can't
Divorce the truth.
Every scar on my soul
Is living proof.

LIVING TO BE A BETTER ME

If I am cordial with mortals,
I might die.
How else can I
Live life literally?
Until I cleanse spiritually,
Death daily,
Until I simply
Love all those
Who hates me,
No ifs and or maybes.
Let these vibrations
Do what they do.
So, now I bring you
Back to your youth.

Not Everything Is for You

I remember the days of
Catching vibrations from elders.
You know when they tell ya
"Stay out of a grown folk conversation,"
When you really just waiting,
Waiting to ask
The most important question
And the answer you need
Before big daddy says blessings.
At that age, it seems like
Time is always pressing,
So, I move to the question:
May I have more than a burger and a hotdog?
Y'all, know I like ribs too
And the catfish.
Oh! oh! oh!
However, my first lesson on truth:
Not everything is meant for you.

The Spoken Truth

Cry Baby Blues

Have you ever pitched pinecones at tree stumps
While swallowing lumps in your throat?
Momma just said no,
And you better not
Ask no more.
Even though you saw her at the store
Purchasing plenty of good meat,
If it's good for you,
Why ain't it good for me?
Sometimes, we are too young to see.
What we got at home
Others don't have in the streets.
So, when the elders come together,
The whole community eats.
Love defeats all, so we can never fall.

The Stand Against Us

In the cold, rough winds,
I hear it again and again,
Victims of ruthless sin
Goosebumps within
Validating history's truth.
With every silent gesture,
There are bold moves,
Bruised egos, and scared souls

THINKING HUMAN
HUMANS THINKING

Hello and welcome to my dimension.
Did I mention
We here in this world
Thrive for analysis,
Not to the point of paralysis,
But to the point
We advocate for the masses.

Power In Me

Who do you really trust?
Ask us,
Meaning me, myself, and I.
Why do you assume the context refers to multiple personalities
And not multiple perspectives?
How and why are you affected by a collection of galaxies
When you actually have billions of stars within yourself?
If you took the time to let yourself shine,
You would find God in yourself.
As a matter of fact,
The truth of our existence may be
Just a poor excuse not to be
Better than what we see.
Is this actually a matter of normalcy?
So, I pose the question:
Is being blind to your potential a part of the human experience?
Are we being serious when we say
We are not all connected?
Don't be so reckless.
I don't know about you,
But I am blessed.

The Spoken Truth

Chapter 2

His Story, Our Pain

My apologies for not really having a plan.
You must understand.
In these emotional times,
We do what we can.
So, it's right here where we
Take this stand
On blood-soiled concrete
Built on blood-soiled sand
In the park next to the school
Where children play hangman,
Using led-filled sticks
Inside brick walls.
They are too young to see the irony.
My grandmother was an eyewitness
To it all.
She watched old trees
Grow new branches,
Just to see them fall
Then grow again.
Just to support the necks of
Black women and black men,
Broken tree branches grow
Again and again.

The Spoken Truth

While these children still play hangmen,
Do you
Understand the example you set?
If your memory does not recollect
Thousands of broken necks,
Thousands of senseless deaths,
Is that a sign of disrespect
Or should I take that as
Your human form has not matured yet?
With every last breath,
With every single step,
I will pray for you to grow and stretch
Until you reach the best you.
The truth is
There are no more lies;
The truth is
We shall and still rise.
So, don't be surprised when you see me
Transcend and fly.
Still, I rise.
Revenge drips from her eyes.
Those lies still linger like the pitch of a bad singer.
Her demeanor looks so concerned.
When will these children learn that
What you did to me
Won't be undone?
My sun,
My moon,
Each stroke of light consumes

My inner voice.
What choice do I have?
What choice was I given?
He and she are living with no reality.
You take and take.
You never asked me.
How am I feeling today?
Hate! Hate! Hate!
I feel it like the greed of your nature.
Wait! Wait! Wait!
No time for later.
The here is now.
I judge you with what you have given.
Giving I am living.
I am life.
I gave you days.
I have given you nights.
I provided your life;
You gave me death.
There is nothing else left.
There is more than enough proof.
Humanity presented its truth.
Now, a mother must do what she must do.
I present to you COVID-19.

WE CONQUERED HAPPINESS

As my memory takes me backward,
These brain cells become active,
Massive reproducing of passive aggression.
Emotions fueled with obsession.
To my recollection,
The only feeling of perfection
Is true happiness.
Happiness is the feeling of no regret.
Self-respect or respecting our self
Because true wealth
Are all the riches inside self.
Increasing mental health
Thru relentless exercise
Brainpower from lifting you and me,
They and them, her and him,
Family and friends.
Yes!
Happiness extends
Beyond our selfish selves.
The fact is
We are compelled to make one another smile.

Let's Connect

Dial up your loving you.
Communicate with your truth.
Look in the mirror,
Beautiful self
Staring right back at you.
Happy you
Is what you do for others.
The smiles you create,
The sadness you smother
For that sister, for that brother.
The fact is
We exist for one another.
Hold each other up,
Up past the sky
That profound question is not why,
Not when, nor how.
It's not a question.
It is the answer we seek.
And it is in
The right now.

Love Yourself To Life

Let's get this straight,
Heavy hearts need not
More weight.
When burdens are heavy,
Don't hesitate.
Take a moment to say,
"We are all far from perfect."
But when you smile,
The earth is reborn
As we rejoice for a new day.
It is not the question.
It is the answer we say,
Followed by what we do
With a smile and a warm heart.
I love you.

We Spirits Of The Galaxies

Waking up to a strange odor,
Funk rising from the third solar,
That's thirty-three degrees off the polar.
Yeah sir.
That's a mouthful
Soul-crushing words.
From the Nebularkian high council
Renders us doubtful of social evolution
Each movement congruent with digression
We are moving forward.
Don't forget your blessings.
Lost spirits are stressing.
Seeds planted moons ago
Are left unprotected.
Hunted by the darkest crows,
But there is still hope.
We are we indeed.
Warriors for peace!
The root of the problem
Will not allow us to leave.
Together we stand.
Breath! Breath! Breath!
I am free.

The Spoken Truth

See me in the distance,
Leader of the Nebularkian resistance
Your smile as my witness,
You the listener
Are highly gifted.

RISE UP HUMAN

While all this time,
Blood stains the memory's surface
Providing soundtracks for serpents.
Lost souls lack purpose.
So, I spit words of encouragement,
Nourishment for the weak soul.
Take hold of this knowledge,
You don't have to go to college.
To understand the hollow words
Screaming at your spirit,
Ears wide shut,
But you still hear it.
Every word, every lyric
You feel it.
I feel it.
Let's deal with the here and now.
Be proud of who you are;
Every spec of melanin is forged from ancient stars.
Listen close.
You heard.
You heard.
You hear God's call.
Rise up, precious human.

The Spoken Truth

Rebels Or Revolutionaries

The other day in Damascus,
Young rebels speaking against fascist
While western masses remain
Medicated and absent.
They lack wits.
 It's real in the field.
No will!
No power!
Weak souls devoured
By words of cowards,
Devils dancing in the witching hour
Like virgins prancing in flowers.
Long time partners
Divided by harder decisions.
Honest intentions
Put good men in prison.
So, these bastards are born sinning.
Youth are misguided and willing.
The enemy is brilliant.
Thinking not is ignorance.
Remain vigilant!
Third-eye vision is essential;
Each decision critical

Protect our seeds from the digital
By speaking emotions into the physical.
Artificial acceptance is pitiful.
False love is what they are giving you.

LOVE IS SERIOUS

Love is not made with some magical fairy dust.
Neither does bearing gifts restore broken trust.
For us to be us,
It is simply a woman's touch,
A touch of understanding,
A touch of virtue.
Meaning behind the words.
Don't make me hurt you.
We've had the stars.
But for now,
The earth will do.

First Glance

As these leaves fall from the trees,
I believe I believe.
It was September.
As I remember,
Our eyes made contact,
Illusions of a perfect match.
As we scratch the surface
Of our very purpose,
Should we continue?
Is it worth it?
Love,
Who will take the chance?
Who will dance the dance?
Memories vividly captured for a lifetime,
A smile or a sigh.
It is neither or never
If we don't try.

Love Me Or Miss Me

My reality is fierce, strong me.
No regrets.
No pity.
Feel me.
Feel my presence.
My relevance is not seen on this earth.
Feel my power throughout the universe.
Each song and verse
Strengthens the earth
Imagine existence without my song.
How?
How?
How will you move on?
I am there when you're alone.
You will miss me when I'm gone.
This is our song.

Nature's Song And Dance

I hear these flowers screaming in the key of G,
Such a brilliant melody.
They tell me flowers don't sing,
But I hear everything,
Especially the ugly truth.
The same thing I'm telling you,
But you don't hear.
How could I be any more sincere?
It's all so clear
Songbirds' senate the seeds of flowers.
I speak the truth to power.
Your ugly lies sour the pedals.
However,
New growth is inevitable.
You can't change the roots.
Can't you hear the flower's song now?
They still sing the truth.

Chapter 3

Thank You Letter

I know I don't say it enough,
Especially when times are rough.
Lately, I've been going through some stuff.
There is no excuse
For my clear abuse of your grace.
It's hard to face facts.
I remember way back,
Back when I was a teenager,
When I most needed a savior,
You showed me favor.
Through all my pathetic attempts,
Flirting with drugs,
To slits on my wrist,
You never missed a moment.
Holding me in your grace,
Your love embraced me
While self-hatred disabled me.
Took penitentiary chances frequently
And you still delivered me.
No, if and or maybe,
You saved me.
You saw through the clay
Since the sixth day.

So, I realize what I must do.
For the situations, you brought me through
And more.
This is for you.
Thank you for all I've been given.
Thank you for my living.
Thank you for your forgiveness.
Thank you for the mountains, the moon, and the stars.
Thank you for who you are.
My father,
Author of the universe,
First and last,
Alpha and omega,
My God,
My savior.
Thank you for all in existence.
Thank you for your magnificence.
I shall strive to do better.
Dear God,
Please forgive me.
For the late thank-you letter.

OPEN ARMS

Suspended in motion,
Still floating like silk in the wind,
My direction depends on
Which way the wind sways.
I begin each day
Suspended in thought,
Caught gliding through every moment.
I owe this to the space we were given.
Hold your head up!
I am still rising above.
Hold your head up!
Watch me swing freely in love,
Gliding through my emotions,
Suspended by devotion.
Hold your head up!
Follow my motions.
Focus!
Focus!
My arms are still open.

STANDING IN THE RAIN

Raindrops piercing my soul,
Cold, wet raindrops strike hard and boldly.
I was told when it rains, it pours.
I stand in the middle of the storm
Waiting for more.
Is that all you got?
My umbrella stops the pain.
Any fella knows I'm not the same old same.
Not just some dame.
Respect my essence.
Respect my name.
I am mother.
I am sister.
I am the piercing cold of the winter,
The heat of the summer.
I am from the dirt of this earth.
I am God's wonder.
I am the calm in the storm.
All be warned!
I ain't afraid.
Before you rain on my parade,
It will only shower.
If or when I say.

Momma Ain't Playing

So, you thought I was all done.
Do you remember where I'm from?
Where I've been?
How this all began?
Me, myself, and I
We made it all possible.
I birthed kings and queens.
I am unstoppable.
Remember when I wiped the tears from your eyes,
Comforted you in your lies,
And gave you life from these thighs.
I gave you the impossible.
You made it this far because I am unstoppable,
Made something from nothing,
Stomach growling,
Nose running,
Tears dripping,
Empty kitchen.
The impossible becomes possible
Because I am unstoppable.
Chin up!
Chest out!
Strength in the words from my mouth.

I mean what I say:
I say what I mean.
Don't make me make a scene.
I am why you're possible.
Your potential is in me.
I am unstoppable.

STRAIGHT TALK PLEASE

I remember us in a different version,
Speaking in the third person,
Flirting with indirect emotions,
Working towards healing,
And still drifting apart like lily pads in ponds.
I am feeling really strong.
I can right these wrongs.
I am the undercurrent pulling toward desire.
My gentle ripples were subtly admired.
This is me,
The new version.
I am still speaking in the third person.
Wait a minute,
What is the purpose of the third person?
We are drifting further and further.
We both shall murder.
Kill the third person!
Kill the third person!
I am quite certain.
You and I
Are one person,
Wholeheartedly.
One version,

A couple in love.
No need to speak in the third person.

You Dirty Cheater

We fell from the comfort of that branch.
How can I forgive you for that?
Suspended in the air by fall leaves.
As these trees exhale life,
We each breathe.
I am caught mesmerized,
Completely hypnotized,
Brilliant life in sight.
With all my might,
I yearn to feel,
Feels like I am real.
We are real.
Is this real?
Still, atmospheres birth blue skies.
Still conciseness birth new lies.
Still, emotions defy common sense.
Reality is realizing.
We are living in the past tense.
Forgive me, my future.
With the past, I have sinned.
For this, I must repent.

BE YOURSELF

Can you hear me?
I am speaking clearly.
Listen up!
I am speaking to your soul.
Bold me with bold words.
Unspoken syllables,
Strike hard and cold.
You sold my affection for cheap thrills.
This is your choice.
This is your will.
Stand still.
Stand in your choice.
Silent screams imitating my voice,
Penetrating the depth of your being.
Are you seeing what I felt?
Are you drowning in your pool of self?
Who is that in your flesh?
This is me in mine.
It's been me since the first time.
Keep hiding miserable you.
I scream for myself.
That's what I'll do.
I found me.

I pray you find yourself.

DIRECTIONS PLEASE

Sitting here pondering which direction,
Left pride right there at the intersection.
I haven't found the map to my affection.
Still wondering throughout life,
I wonder if I was right.
I left at the height of our descent.
It's all downhill now.
Should I still vent?
Hot air blowing from my lungs.
As I wonder, far from,
Far from our beginnings.
Still wondering!
Still thinking!
I wonder what we believe in.
I left you right there again,
In the past.
Still moving forward,
No matter the path.
It was the right decision.
I left the past.

I'm Not Perfect; I'm Strong

Silver linings defining outcomes,
I see beyond this situation.
My preparation is ongoing.
I was hoping you give me grace.
My face was stained with redemption;
My heart pierced with conviction.
I have all the ingredients.
Ain't nothing missing!
Give me more of your bad intentions.
This fire burning inside me is intuition.
You better make your decision.
I'm cooking up a batch of strength,
Served with a good old celebration.
I ain't there yet,
But I still made it,
Made it this far.
When you are sitting on the moon,
You shot past the stars.
So, give me all you got.
I have already made it this far.

TOO MUCH NOISE

It's probably better we don't talk.
Just hold my hand and take a walk.
The tensions are
As noisy as they ever were.
Your intentions are clear as bright red rose buds.
Love.
Is it still in your subconscious?
Can you hear it?
Is it still obvious?
Throughout the cloudy days, I feel the sun.
When the rain pours, I feel the warmth.
I do, and you don't.
Why don't you?
Is it true?
Is the noise more pleasing than our music?
I was your instrument of desire.
So, you just abused it.
Useless words with no feelings,
Your ignorance simply magnifies my brilliance.

Chapter 4

VICTIMS DON'T DIE, WE SURVIVE TO FIGHT

Victims don't die, we multiply.
Your filthy sins struck deep inside.
You struck my spirit.
However, my soul survived.
Time heals the ill.
But we won't forget.
Wipe that smug smile away,
Or I'll get my wish.
I wish you feel what I've felt,
What was done to me
Be done to yourself.
Your poor decision did not affect my wealth.
I am rich in gratification.
I spoke for a complete generation.
Irritating nay-sayers.
Knocking down giants.
Igniting strength in others with beautiful defiance.
Your reliance on me always has been.
I stand firm.
Hear me roar!

Confessions Of A Human

Still waters caressing the muddy surface,
Gentle ripples serving a single purpose,
The calm before the turbulence.
From the still pond emerges bliss,
Happiness from my perspective,
Complete satisfaction from my recollection.
These are my confessions.
I confess I'm blessed in times of stress.
I confess each breath is a gift.
Confess my weakness is my strength.
I confess what matters most
Is this very moment.
So, seize it and own it.
Splash!
Splash!

Gaslighting My Love

Don't speak to me,
Speak to my vengeance.
Relentless pursuit of endless retribution.
You clumsy fool,
What were you doing?
Your awkward balance broke my heart.
You fell in the dark.
I turned on the lights.
There I saw you with my heart.
No balance.
Crisscrossing on a tightrope,
Gripping my heart like life depended on it.
At that moment, it was hard to breathe.
So, I rolled up my sleeves,
Then took it back.
This ain't no circus act.
My heart ain't to be played with.
Now, go on back there and pack your trash.

My Dedication

This morning felt a bit odd,
Not an average day on the job.
My human interactions
Brought me closer to God,
Collaboration through embracing
Our shared reality.
Actually, I was not expecting this.
With no warning, we unite.
Our distance is only facilitated by the night.
Bright days ahead, and right
Were left, moving forward to new heights.
New existence with persistence.
We take flight.
One team, one fight.
I might share my emotions.
We are spiritually connected to our devotion.
Devoted to more than self,
Devoted to mental health,
Devoted to helping others,
Devoted to staying on pace,
Dedicated to helping the human race.

DON'T FORGET ME

Knowledge is knowing I am not sin-free.
Knowledge is finding out about the most flawed me.
Wisdom is just letting me be.
Who's the real me?
The secrecy between myself, I, and me.
The sinful man.
Not perfect to any degree.
Wisdom is knowing not to put too much faith in myself.
Wisdom is knowing only God is perfect.
Put too much faith in me,
God may put me beneath the surface.
Wisdom is understanding the turbulence.
Wisdom is understanding those rough times bring us closer to being perfect.
The experience we pass on,
The emotions made us strong.
Not the words we read,
Not the illusions we see.
If seeing is believing,
What do you see?
What have you experienced?
Wisdom is in the important things we remember.
Will you remember me?

Where I'm From

Where I'm from,
I'm not sure where I should begin.
However, I was born from sin.
She's yearning for it.
She got to have it.
Repercussions of a habit,
Momma was an addict.
Daddy was far-gone.
At the age of 6 months,
I was left alone.
My brother was 4 years old, keeping me alive.
Toilet water in a bottle helped me survive.
I still got the paperwork.
I ain't telling no lies.
"Property of the state"
Until adoption.
You would think my past life distorted my options,
However, there is no stopping destiny.
Screw negativity!
My trials and tribulations
Made a better me.
It is how it's
Because that's the way

It's supposed to be.
So, hopefully, you don't feel any sorrow.
The past is the past.
Let's work on tomorrow.
Oh yeah, you asked where I'm from.

Objects Of Desire

I saw it as a child.
It grows wild in our imagination,
Anticipating what is waiting in adulthood.
I should speak less and listen.
We would hear the tension.
I would hear the disgust.
We would feel vibrations of mistrust.
Just look at us,
We learned to admire stuff,
Nothing but invisible currency.
That paper ain't worth nothing to me.
Why is it worth it to you?
I guess you lost the truth.
Back when I was innocent,
Too young to know I must repent.
I never saw one red cent.
Happiness was abundant.
Love was redundant.
Something went so wrong,
No worries though.
It won't be long now.
Well, get back to the ancestor's ways.
My lineage.

The Spoken Truth

Our lineage.
Can you still feel it?
God is right here with us.

I Can See That

In between balance and falling,
There is a perfect spot.
Still uncomfortable on top,
Not prepared to drop.
It's right there in between.
Seldom seen because it's hiding in plain sight.
When did we become so uncomfortable with the truth?
Wise words need no proof.
Lies hide right in front of you.
Comfortable, ain't it?
It's so amazing
That level of our ignorance
Don't laugh at innocence.
It will prevail in happy moments.
First, find out where you are going,
Then you will see what you've left.
Truth!

I Will Argue With Me Until I'm Better

Today, I found myself speaking out of turn.
I guess I got what I deserved,
Loud voices replying with aggressive overtones.
These words hit home.
What's wrong with talking to yourself anyway?
Any other day I would say
I'm tired of the doubt.
What are you talking about anyway?
We've been at this
Since I can remember.
We are still with you,
Mind, spirit, and soul.
So, what if we are separate?
You just don't get it.
Who says we have to be whole,
Separate but with equal rights?
One day, we might
Meet in the flesh
When you learn self-respect,
When you learn to forgive,
When you learn to forget.
I will drop you a line later;

The three of us should connect.

THE POWER IN ME

Your mortal thoughts cannot curse me.
My ancestors begged for your mercy.
Mind and body enslaved perfectly.
We certainly came from the mud.
My blood still reeks of oppression.
While you offer your human suggestions,
I need not your confessions.
My first impression was at Antioch Baptist Church,
Choir singing with the angels.
Pastor Edwards is at work.
I know where I came from,
I know who I'm with.
My strength,
My purpose,
My blessings,
My direction,
Are straight from God?
So, I ask you with an open mind,
With wide open ears.
How do you think we survived four hundred years?
The answer is clear.
God, oh mighty God!
Jah!

Chapter 5

I Can't Hate You

You humans still don't get it.
Conscious ignorance is not brilliance.
Your hate is an addiction.
Where are your emotions?
Where are your feelings?
Self-centered you can't see destiny.
Take what you will,
You can't take the best of me.
My spirit.
My soul.
I am God's child.
I will love you boldly.

Nobody Is Perfect

I see serpents speaking in code,
Bold gestures welcoming conflict.
We sit, watch, and pray.
Hopefully, one day, they will see
See past me into the truth.
I am you,
You are me.
You and I should be the same person.
I was born again.
I am a new version.
You chose death.
Darkness is still lurking.
Yes, I know.
Nobody is perfect.
But if we try,
The effort is worth it.

MESSAGE TO MY PEOPLE

Black boy walking around in a fishbowl,
I see you when it's hot;
I see you when it's cold.
Day and night,
Black boy in a fishbowl,
I see when you steal;
I see when you cry.
I always see you.
Don't you tell that lie!
Black boy, don't you know
The fishbowl lets us see it all?
When you rise to the top,
We watch you fall.
Y'all don't get it.
The behavior you mimic,
Each and every gimmick,
All designed to keep you in that fishbowl.
It's not your fault though.
You were bred for that.
We are scared of you for being that.
You ain't threatening in that fishbowl though.
Look at him grow.
Look at him go.

We all see you in that fishbowl.
You're so comfortable.
What would you live for?
You got it all inside that fishbowl.
We see you.

Taking Responsibility

Yes sir,
I'm still waiting on that old check.
Maybe when it comes,
I'll buy some self-respect
Or maybe I'll buy shoes.
I wasn't taught to invest in myself.
I think I'll invest in you.
What else do you do
When it's your version of the truth
I've been given.
My truth never made it.
It was lost somewhere between greed and hatred.
This sounds far fetch.
Sounds like it ain't even possible.
Sounds like it is not plausible.
With each breath flowing in and out of my nostrils,
Lungs expanding beneath my flesh,
I do confess.
There is a dereliction of duty.
We must truly be fools.
If we think,
They and them,
Me and you

Life Written in Poetry

Are not responsible for ourselves.

LOOKING FOR LOVE & FINDING LOVE ADDICTION

I remember being addicted to the tribe,
Connected to the lives
In my circumference,
My brothers and I constantly hunted.
Who did it?
Who done it?
The typical vocabulary of the hunter.
We were baptized
In the sins of our mothers.
My brothers and I,
We scream ride or die.
Die knowing the love of the tribe
What we felt inside.
Temporary emotions fill the void,
Rejoicing in false thoughts,
Caught mourning the life before,
Freedom should not be a dream
Trapped inside our conscience.
God will set us free.

MESSAGE TO YOU READING THIS

No such thing as perfect,
You, the reader.
You are totally worth it;
Faults and all.
Stand tall and be you.
Live your truth.
The secret really is love.
Love is the key to humanity.
Understandably,
If we didn't hate,
We would all live together for free,
No imaginary currency prostituting our souls,
Just helping hands helping hands,
No lost souls enduring the cold.
Then again, truth is simplicity.
You really should examine those lies.
I mean we should really examine our lives.

WE SURE LOVE OUR JOBS, DON'T WE?

Dependent on fancy titles for our survival,
I, for one,
Would choose a name from the bible like
Moses, Isaac, Noah, or Jacob,
Place it
Right at top of my mind.
The next time I apply for a job.
While I'm praying to God,
I get hired.
Looking for fancy titles to admire,
I'll inquire.
How much pain can I sell my soul for?
Is it still worth it?

MESSAGE TO THE OPPRESSED

The revolution is simply God's truth
Manifested in this human form.
There is no ignoring the vibrations
Of ancestors celebrating us.
Finding God in us.
My lord, let the blind see the rhythm.
Let the deaf hear it deep down.
Each and every sound.
Those who are lost,
It's time to get found.
Head barely above water
But we never drown.
We became amphibious.
If you are curious,
That's why the drip stays wet,
Gills creating possibilities
For new breath
While these scales protect us from the element.
The relevance of this dialogue
Is deep in your soul,
Where your spirit hovers around.
It is there where ancient mothers are found
Whispering righteous words of ancient.

Let's face it,
We are fighting to keep
Those memories alive.
Memories are how we survive.
Memories are ancestors never forgotten.
Still speaking through memories,
Vividly painting the truth,
Even if you've destroyed and erased the truth,
You now know
What they already knew.
Let's call it the new school.
If you erase my past,
You destroy my ability
To speak freely on behalf of my elders.
If you simply knew better,
You would do better.
It's getting cold out here,
Grab yourself a sweater.
I hope it ain't cotton.

WE ARE SCARED OF THE LAW

Just in case you were wondering,
It was never forgotten.
I am so tired of traveling
Back to the
Memory of a young boy,
With his face pruned
Staring at Godzilla's
Reflection in the moon.
If I make an ass of you and me,
Then I assume I will soon
Face the music,
However,
Standing in front of bars
Is not my idea of amusement.
So, I restrict every movement,
Staying still as pond water
While I sit and ponder.
Why I should honor
Your authority?
There is more to me
Than you will ever know.
As I grow back up,
At the moment,

The Spoken Truth

I begin to regain focus
From receiving atrocious
Treatment.
My shaken spirit settling from its decent
Back from the
Child in me.
Glad I can
Still feel and see
Some folks take this trip
With a flip of a switch.
They are restricted from the right to breathe.
So, I thank God
For my return.
Buttocks still firm
In this seat,
Hands at 11 and one
While our eyes meet,
"No worries, officer."
You won't have any problems with me.
If I can
Just have a moment,
I need a second to breathe.
It's so hard to see
Past the fear.
I wish I could say
I wasn't going
Back there again.
However,
As long as I am breathing,

You will always challenge my freedom.
So, next time I return back
To my child-like state
Where it seems so safe
Not to be a threat,
I promise
I won't forget
To say,
"Officer, please have
A nice day."

Chapter 6

I Wrote You A Letter

The time it takes
To write a letter,
What a better expression of love.
The written word,
Who is it from?
Someone who took the time
Listen to me and read mine.
Dear reader,
God loves you.
You are completely worth it.
Hold your head up.
Nobody is perfect.
Let go and let God
Every time you feel turbulence.
Sincerely yours,
You're still worth it.

I Saw The Truth

Standing in the mirror,
It becomes clearer.
I see happiness
At the tip of my nose
I suppose.
Smelling freedom is far-fetched.
Goosebumps on my flesh
Indicate honesty in my reflection.
I am happy with myself.
I am a blessing.

A Bit Too Heavy

You're still carrying that weight,
All that you've got inside.
I would offer you a ride,
But there's no room for baggage.
How do you carry it all?
How do you manage
Carrying that baggage
Every place you go?
Slow down for a minute.
See what's holding you up.
That's too much weight.
I'd help you store a bit,
But there's no room
At my place.
That luggage ain't pretty,
Not one bit.
If you would just
Open one bag at a time,
You'd see nothing fits.
You outgrew it
A long time ago.
Do yourself a favor.
Don't carry these bags anymore.

SMILE, PLEASE

Smiling is a beautiful gesture.
It takes no pressure.
At the right moment,
It makes a day better.
Have you ever seen
Scowling faces embrace laughter?
In those moments of anger,
What really matters?
Selfishness or ego
Is so important.
When do we let go?
What do we really know
About ourselves?
When will we prevail?
Triumph over self.
Death to our worst quality.
Life obviously makes us smile.
So, can I see your best you?

Sun Rise

Looking out the window at cloudy skies,
Fog piercing my eyes
Waiting for the sunrise,
My son is up.
So, daddy replies,
"Good morning my son,
May you shine on
Until the
Star deck heaven pierces the atmosphere."
When darkness is as near
As it gets,
And the moon spits
Glimmers of light
With less radiant beams.
But they always seem
To hold until we
Rise again,
With a thank you
And an amen.
I say again,
"What say you, free man?"
If you feel free,
Then you are who you are.

The Spoken Truth

Like I say, "I am who I am."
Of course, you understand.
The plan is
We must rise
And walk in this light
With every ray of hope.
Let there always be warmth
When we travel these roads,
Like goodbye and hello,
From west to east
Or whichever way you go.

Thank You Prayer

Dear heavenly father,
Author of the universe,
Thank you for this earth.
Thank you for this life.
Thank you for the right to breathe.
Thank you for shining your light on me,
Even if I ain't perfect.
You always forgive me,
Even when I feel I ain't worth it.
Let the sunshine and the moonlight
Continue to illuminate my surface,
Exposing all serpents in my path.
Amen.

SOMETHING ABOUT TIME

Just sitting here,
Watching time,
It's all mine.
Yeah, I own my time.
So, I'm like
It's my time,
Now or never.
What could be better
Than
I or me.
Finally getting up off my intentions
And following my intuition.
Right now, I should
Follow my vision,
But I've been feeling
Just a little blue
Talking to me,
Like I'm not you
When you are in me.
Eyes wide shut;
I can't see
Not until I
Take the time

To at least breathe.
I'm in rare form.
Let me spread my wings
See how time flies.
By the way,
I like taking my time.
Giving it to you
Is probably not wise.
So, I will spend it wisely.
Slow life down a bit
So, it doesn't pass
By me.
Oh, did I mention
I've been meaning too
Ask this question?
Before I forget,
What time is it?

Them Good Ol' Church Days

The other day I was thinking about way back,
Back to the days of butterfly-collared shirts and tube socks
Passing by manipulating thugs on my way up the block,
Heading to Antioch Missionary Baptist Church,
Sunday School was cool.
But I came to see Reverend Edwards go to work,
Preaching and whooping, whooping and preaching.
I think he is reaching deep down and waking up someone's soul.
Somebody probably still sleeps.
From the Sunday before last and the one before that,
Hold up one sec.
Let me take a step back.
They say children see the truth.
I grew up so fast.
I must have missed the proof.
What I see he and she do
Look like somebody ain't telling the truth.
It doesn't matter to me, and it shouldn't matter to you.
We come to do one thing.
Let your praise ring!
Let the church sing!
All praise to the king!

All praise to the creator!
All praise to the father!
Author of the universe.
He has seen me at my worse,
When I was lost.
He sent a search party for my rescue.
Let me tell you,
I was gone for a minute,
But now, I'm back.
I'm still praying, "God, help keep me on track."
So, I pray for His strength.
So, I can do just that.
And as a matter of fact,
I'll pray the same for you.
Love is the truth.
The truth is love.
The proof came from above
And died on the cross for the lost.
Our father sacrificed His only son.
That is love.
And love is God.

Message From My Ancestors Through Me To You

I still hear the rhythm of my ancestors' heartbeats,
Beating to the rhythm of my destiny,
Enticing the best of me
To outperform your spoon-fed mediocracy.
Obviously, there are a few issues to resolve.
"My God, help me through this."
I still hear the sound of lost slaves speaking in fluid pain.
Their worst nightmare still remains.
We proudly accept whips in chains.
So put that leather to you back in the whip,
While your gold chain hangs
Right there around your neck.
The genocides on autopilot.
You're killing yourself.
Wake up and overstand it.
I hear the heartbeat of slave souls
Trapped in the Atlantic,
Whispering to the masses.
Silent screams, yelling "Move forward,"
While we keep moving backward.
Silent screams, yelling the secret.

We are still kings and queens.
Remember one thing,
You are the king and queen of your galaxy.
You're actually the birth of a new star system.
Each and every organism gives birth to another
All connected to mother earth.
Oh, you king you,
Oh, you queen you,
Let's do what we do.
And vibrate to the rhythm of our ancestors' heartbeats.
We must complete the supreme architect's assignment.
Rely on the creator and king
And they can never divide us.
How do you think we survived over 400 years?
He was with us then,
And he is still here.
Come home earth child,
The tribe awaits you.
Yah!

Chapter 7

Days Of Our Lives

I'm so thankful for today.
Like I appreciate tomorrow.
So, let's agree to free these burdens.
Let's pull the curtains on sorrow.
These are just
The days of our lives.
We strive to say alive.
So, we can see
Another moment in time.
We have the power to define
Each and every emotion.
Devoting our time
To what matters most.
So, what matters to you?
What will you do
With your piece of time?
Will you waste it
Crying over the past,
Crying over a present you don't deserve?
You can gift yourself.
So, give yourself the present you deserve,
And the future too.

The Spoken Truth

Everything you do
Has cause and effect.
Why don't you select a piece of positivity?
It's really not that hard.
Set yourself apart from
What you think you deserve
And take what's yours.
You own your happiness.
So, get up!
It is time to get active.
Imagine who you could be,
Now look in the mirror.
Can you see
You are that human already?
So, get ready!
There's no turning back.
The fact is
Your
Imperfections are beautiful.
You are perfectly suitable for royalty,
So, soar with me
To the highest heights.
And PS,
Quit counting likes.

THAT OLD PIANO PLAYING LIFE'S TUNES

I wish I had an old piano
Clunking along to the
Rhythm of life.
With a painful melody and
Odd synths sound telling me,
"Stay in tune and have patience,
Soon, the waiting will be over."
As the rhythm section
Struggles under deep currents,
These thoughts become verses
Drowning in gut-wrenching purpose.
This work is never done.
Some folks say,
Before you can
Truly live life,
You must wrestle with despair;
The who, the what
And why you should care.
This gut-wrenching human experience
Is something serious.
I am not at all curious,

Not at all surprised.
When I see grey clouds raping blue skies,
Leaving pain dripping all over humanity.
Understandably, I was built for these types of blues.
My shoes were made to walk in misery.
Y'all ain't hearing me.
This complexion attracts tyranny,
Like my reflection packs empathy.
If you don't believe me,
You should be embarrassed.
My ancestors stood in the face of Jim Crow terrorist
With undeniable courage.
I'm talking honesty in the face of hatred.
I'm talking, "I love you in the face of a racist."
I couldn't make this up.
Like you can't erase it.
I'm simply saying, "Don't believe the lies."
We all will rise,
Like this 15-year-old nappy-headed kid in
A white tee and Levi's,
Sipping St. Ides
Believing lies from the uniformed;
Now grown up and strong in my belief.
Knowing the knotty head thug is still beneath
This unperfect flesh.
So, join me in a toast.
Toast to the death of our foolish selves and rebirth into the revolution.

LOVE AT FIRST SIGHT

Hello,
I've been watching your profile
From across the room,
And I assume
Our acquaintance will lead to forever.
I'm talking for better or worse.
At least, that's what I was thinking
While drinking this cup of water,
Working up the nerves just to speak.
We've never met,
And I am scared to meet
The woman of my dreams.
It seems like I am holding myself back.
I can't ignore the fact that
My self-esteem seems to be running low.
I took a few fatal blows
In this game of love and war.
And why love has been war,
I'll never know.
So, if you shoot me down,
I'll be back for more.
I know. I know. I know.

The Spoken Truth

We have never met before,
But if and when we do,
The truth is
You will have all of me.
Sincerely yours,
The Facebook stalker.

SURVIVING THE BREAKUP

I'm still catching feelings,
Oh yeah.
I'm still catching feelings,
Catching feelings from the first time.
The first time I felt pain,
The first time I felt pleasure,
The first time I felt better.
Standing next to my
Favorite human being,
Seeing myself in a future context,
Wondering what my next move was.
What can and what should I do
To keep on
Feeling this feeling.
Until the moment I was
Okay never seeing you again,
Thinking to myself,
We are better when
We are apart.
So far apart,
I can't feel the pain anymore.
It seems like,

It rains more when
Your heart is aching,
When your stomach is
Tied in knots,
When you can't stop
Thinking of that other human.
Oh, excuse me.
I'm assuming y'all have been in love before.
If you ever walked through that door,
It's totally worth it.
Love is so perfect.
Humans are so flawed.
After all, we expect to get it all
With no expectations of giving.
Someone has to be willing,
Willing to sacrifice,
Sacrifice because it is worth it.
If humans sacrifice for each other,
The love continues to be perfect
Like we continue to be flawed.
So, let's celebrate love.
Because it is better to love once
Than to never have loved at all.

Humans United Defying And Ignoring Differences

I must start by
Asking a question of us,
"How in the hell
Could we send
Good vibrations
From the back of the bus?"
"How much suffering must one endure
Before pure hate
Initiates the opposition?"
Not to mention
400 years of lynching,
I apologize if I
Keep my distance
When you assume I should forget
What was forgiven.
We love the human and hate the sinner,
Like some folk just
Love the man and hate the brother.
So, let me rap you a tune.
So, you can assume

I'll never be any bigger.
No worries.
I hate the sin,
But I love the sinner.
That's simply what it means
To be human.
While you're sitting there
Consuming the pain,
I will toss it to the side.
There's nothing to gain from
Hatred and ill feelings.
Nothing but ulcers and high blood pressure.
We are better when we love.
Come on y'all.
How do you think we made it so far?
The weight was always heavy.
So, we raised the bar.
So, you dumbbells can make it this far.
It takes repetition.
Duplicate your ancestral decisions.
Duplicate your business.
That means
Repetitive ambitions,
Double down on intuition,
Cultivate your vision.
This is our chance.
Get up out of your feelings!
We are one
Living organism,

Vibrating within this sphere.
If I wasn't clear,
You are not feeling.
You are not willing.
Everybody quit hating.
These moments are fading.
We humans could be so amazing.
But it's like that,
So, let me tell you,
It is time, my black.
We must connect back
With our consciences.
Humans are all the same.
There is nothing opposite.

The Spoken Truth

Voices Of Generations

Hi, hello, and yes, I know.
This is that familiar vibe.
Sort of like days of our lives,
When we all subject to lies.
And lies are the subject.
Who stands among us
In this republic
Without just cause
To bear arms like
Bodybuilders in tank tops.
Of course, there's more crime
When you punish the good cops,
Reduce the size of the force.
So, who's going to patrol your blocks?
Y'all must have forgotten,
Like cheetahs,
You can't change your spots.
The rent went high.
They want a whole lot.
"Object" is to move you off your block.
Hi, crime is cheap property.
Buy low and obviously, sell high.

No peace for the genocide movement.
It is congruent with gentrification.

You Can't Hide Pain, So Ask For Help

Hello and greetings earthlings,
We are beginning this journey with a purpose.
Before we depart,
How may I be of service?
May I remove that circus smile?
You worked hard to paint that mask on.
But I see through it right now.
So, let your pain go.

MESSAGE TO OURSELVES

I never knew
I would be speaking to you,
Telling you to live your dreams,
Telling you are worth it,
Like nobody is perfect,
Like everyone is worth it,
Like failure is a lie,
Nobody ever fails.
We just learn to
Try a bit differently.
What's meant for us,
We will get it.
If it's not meant for you,
That means there is something bigger.
Sorry for the change in dialogue,
But your life is worth
Changing direction in this poem.
I hope this hit home.
Like an unexpected storm,
Let it transform you into the new you.
I hope you get it.

The Spoken Truth

Chapter 8

SOUNDTRACK FOR MOVEMENT

Excuse me while I
Enjoy the hi of this rhythm,
While feeling this bass deep in my soul,
While these guitar licks stroll,
Right into my life.
Like a sweet melody caressing my every thought.
While I'm caught somewhere between lost and found.
Yeah, I've been down this road plenty.
I know some of y'all are right there with me,
Sincerely, you're just human.
I'm assuming y'all get it.
So, let me stress this message.
Life is yours, so get up and go get it.
There ain't no rollover minutes when you finish, you finish.
If you haven't got it by now, you better get up and get it.
This is that spoken word.
You know the one that gets you up.
Do you think you can move forward?
Don't let time pass.
Catch this moment.
Reach and grab it.
Hold on and don't let go.

The Spoken Truth

There is more to know;
There is more to do.
There is more of me,
Like there is more to you.
It's time to make it do what it does.
You are far from through.
Your new beginning is "do."
You are not a statue.
It's time to make moves.
I'm not preaching at you.
I'm just speaking the truth.
This poem took a turn.
So, this message could reach you.

BUILDING SELF ESTEEM

While contemplating the fact about
How time keeps on moving faster,
I am distracted by
The crows' laughter.
Every day I say about
Seven or eight
The morning after
My fractured emotions were
Soaking up the past tense.
Keeping my future in suspense.
Sort of like
Rinse and repeat,
Knowing I should never
Admit defeat.
I should always stand on my feet.
Ten toes to the earth,
And know my worth.
Because I am
To die for.
That's one fact
I cannot ignore.
Do you believe that

Dirty sinner me
Is worthy of
Death for my mistakes?
The ultimate sacrifice
For my fate.
Well, let me say,
Y'all know I was Fina preach.
There's been a bad connection.
Y'all are so hard to reach.
Like kids with no eyes and ears
Are so hard to teach,
Maybe I should just
Let y'all be.
Nah! never that.
I'm trying to
Break y'all free.
So, here's your chance.
Don't let advanced social science
Silence your history.

I Remember Words
Of The Ancestors

This ain't no mystery.
The past is not
Visibly pleasing.
My ancestors remain relevant,
Like my God is the past, the future, and the present.
So, God is always relevant.
Let them tell it.
They call us monkeys with no tails.
Let me tell it.
You are goin' feel it is like braille.
Let the truth prevail.
Let freedom yell
At the top of Mt Rushmore
Where former slave owners
Stare with a stone face.
That means
Your history remains in place,
But no worries,
God's got a place for me in His kingdom.
So, I'm still singing at the mountain top.

I'm Only Human

Hello, my humans.
It's time to get down,
Get down to the sound of victory,
Like the keys are so smooth,
And this bass is so filthy.
This heart is so smooth.
And this flesh is so filthy.
I'm a born sinner.
Are you right here with me?
Every day, I'm looking for victory.
There is no sensor in my life.
I'm exposed to it all.
I pray I stand tall
In the midst of sin.
The next day I'm back on my knees again,
Praying for one victory at a time.
Still praying I win.
Praying I celebrate more than I repent,
We all have knots, twists, and dents.
Thank God I can't afford the tents.
So, when you see me vent,
I'm just coolin' off.

COVID HAD ME TRIPPING

Please forgive me.
I literally feel like I am
Lost in some sort of movie
Where every actor seems too foolishly
Repeat all types of tom-foolery
While shoving off to the sea with nothing to guide me.
But your forgiveness
That's metaphorically written
To describe this hurting
Behind these curtains,
I've been this person
I've never known.
Maybe it's all this time
We have spent at home,
Hiding from imminent doom.
June's almost back again.
Please forgive me.
I'm climbing back up from my descent,
To find myself in the same spot when
I was still asking to be forgiven,
All in my feelings,

The Spoken Truth

Like public pools in the summertime,
Before murdering plagues
Turned time against some
While others adapted to overcome.
Now back to whence I came,
So, you can see where I am coming from,
See what I have done,
Or see what I did.
Either way, we are all kids in this universe,
For better or worse.
So, keep it moving.
Are you a human "just being,"
Or a human "just doing?"
Please forgive me.
If my thought patterns,
Keep you moving,
Either your chasing
Or you are pursuing.
No matter what,
Forgive yourself.
We all have room for improvement.

PEACE UPON THE EARTH CHILDREN

Greetings earth children,
I come to take you to a place
Where you will be acknowledged for your brilliance,
Your beautiful defiance
Has not been forgotten.
I represent the Nebularkian high council.
About four hundred years ago,
We came in black earth suits;
Our earthly bodies suffered for all of you.
Every color, every sister, every brother.
We hoped your human race would discover
The meaning of life.
As we watched you steal, kill, bicker, and fight,
We prayed and prayed.
You would discover life.
But you chose pain,
Again and again.
Hatred spewing from your existence,
No repentance for your sins,
You women, you men,
You have not been honest.

The Spoken Truth

So, the forgotten promise
Will fulfilled like this.
Earth children and allies
Come aboard my spaceship.
It's time for a trip into the future.
You are stuck in time.
Now, I must move you.

THE FLIGHT

As the star deck, heaven surrounds us,
Stardust massages the ship's surface.
The closer we get to our purpose,
We begin to understand
The sacrifice was worth it.
You and I were always flirting with destiny
While others fell victim
To intergalactic felonies.
We selfishly gave our love for peace.
I still hear the vibrations telling me,
Don't let the love cease.
So, we continue ducking black holes, and time sucks,
Hoping the ship won't be crushed.
We are on time, no need to rush.
Enjoy the flight.
We don't have to go back to the future
To make things right.
We've left the earth's atmosphere.
Moving forward,
Set the ship's destination to forgiveness.
We won't be back to visit pain.
I'm not sorry.

The Spoken Truth

I won't see you again.
I'm sorry; you didn't see your potential.
We were always we.
There was never the individual.

FINDING ANOTHER TRUTH

In these walls of frequencies,
I find comfort in vibrations,
Navigating temptations frequently.
The situation is equally important
As the last conversation with self.
The conversation where I found wealth
In the knowledge of self.
The conversation where I found life in God,
Where I found death in sin.

Made in the USA
Las Vegas, NV
19 December 2022